W0081531

What Jobs Do They Do?

by Jimena Reyes

 NATIONAL GEOGRAPHIC LEARNING CENGAGE Learning

Every day you go to school.
You read, you write, and you play, too.
Other people go to work.
What do these people do?

This person works with pets.
She works with quite a few.
She always helps sick animals.
What does this person do?

3

This woman is a vet!

She takes care of cats and dogs.
She even helps sick birds and goats,
and horses, sheep, and frogs!

vet

This person works with a stove.
He makes good food for you.
This person uses pots and pans.
What does this person do?

This man is a chef!

You can see him in his kitchen.
He cooks pizza, fish, and eggs,
and soup with rice and chicken.

chef

This person wears a special hat.
His coat is special, too.
He goes to work in a truck.
What does this person do?

This man is a firefighter!

He's ready all day long
to fight fires and help people.
He's very big and strong.

firefighter

8

When you are feeling sick,
this person takes care of you.
She's often at a hospital.
What does this person do?

This woman is a doctor!

She listens to your heart.
A nurse often helps her.
She's really very smart.

doctor

There are so many different jobs.
These jobs are just a few.
Someday when you grow up,
what do you want to do?

dentist

soccer player

bus driver

pilot

Facts About Dog Workers

Did you know that some animals have jobs, too? They are not bus drivers, dentists, or pilots. But they do work. Here are some jobs that dogs do.

Some dogs help people in danger.

Some dogs take care of other animals.

Some dogs help people who can not see.

Some dogs are even movie stars!

Some dogs pull sleds across the snow.

13

Fun with Jobs

Draw a line to match.

chef

bus driver

firefighter

doctor

vet

Write the name of each worker.

nurse   pilot   chef   movie star

1. _____pilot_____

2. _____

3. _____

4. _____

Glossary

heart

hospital

pans

pets

pots

sick